Space Leftovers

A Book About Comets, Asteroids, and Meteoroids

by Dana Meachen Rau   illustrated by Denise Shea

PICTURE WINDOW BOOKS
Minneapolis, Minnesota

Thanks to our advisers for their expertise, research, and advice:

Dr. Stanley P. Jones, Assistant Director
NASA-sponsored Classroom of the Future Program

Susan Kesselring, M.A., Literacy Educator
Rosemount–Apple Valley–Eagan (Minnesota) School District

Editorial Director: Carol Jones
Managing Editor: Catherine Neitge
Creative Director: Keith Griffin
Editor: Christianne Jones
Story Consultant: Terry Flaherty
Designer: Joe Anderson
Page Production: Picture Window Books
The illustrations in this book were created digitally.

Picture Window Books
5115 Excelsior Boulevard
Suite 232
Minneapolis, MN 55416
877-845-8392
www.picturewindowbooks.com

Printed in the United States of America.

Library of Congress Cataloging-in-Publication Data
Rau, Dana Meachen, 1971-
Space leftovers : a book about comets, asteroids, and meteoroids / by Dana Meachen Rau;
illustrated by Denise Shea.
p. cm. — (Amazing science)
Includes bibliographical references and index.
ISBN 1-4048-1137-0 (hardcover)
1. Comets—Juvenile literature. 2. Asteroids—Juvenile literature. 3. Meteoroids—Juvenile
literature. 4. Solar system—Juvenile literature. I. Shea, Denise, ill. II. Title. III. Series.

QB721.5.R385 2006
523.6—dc22   2005003728

Table of Contents

Floating Leftovers

What a big meal! There are sandwiches, fruit, pretzels, and lemonade. There is even dessert! One person can't eat all of this food. There will surely be leftovers.

Did you know there are leftovers floating in space? These leftovers are not pretzels or apple slices. They are pieces of rock, dust, and ice.

FUN FACT

There are three types of space leftovers: comets, asteroids, and meteoroids. They are part of the solar system. The solar system includes a star and the planets that circle around it.

Gas and Dust

Billions of years ago, the solar system started as a big cloud of gas and dust. Gases and dust float in space.

How did this cloud become the solar system? Some bits of gas and dust clumped together, grew hot, and made the sun. Other bits clumped together and made the planets. The leftover pieces of gas, dust, and ice formed asteroids, comets, and meteoroids. These objects are often called space rocks.

FUN FACT
The sun is the center of the solar system. The planets travel around the sun. Some are made of rock. Some are made of gas.

Little Planets

What are the pieces of rock and metal that orbit the sun with the planets? These pieces are asteroids. Many of them travel around the sun on a path between the orbit paths of Mars and Jupiter.

There are millions of asteroids. Some people call them little planets, or minor planets, because they orbit like the planets.

FUN FACT

Some asteroids are close to Earth. They are called Near-Earth Asteroids. People watch the paths of Near-Earth Asteroids closely. These people check to see if the Earth's orbit and the Near-Earth Asteroids' orbits will ever cross.

Icy Visitors

Do you have friends and family who live far away?
Do they come to visit?

Icy balls called comets are visitors from far away. Most comets come from the edge of the solar system. They travel in an orbit that takes them close to the sun. Then they go around the sun and back to where they started. It's a long trip. Some comets visit every four years. Others visit only once every 30 million years!

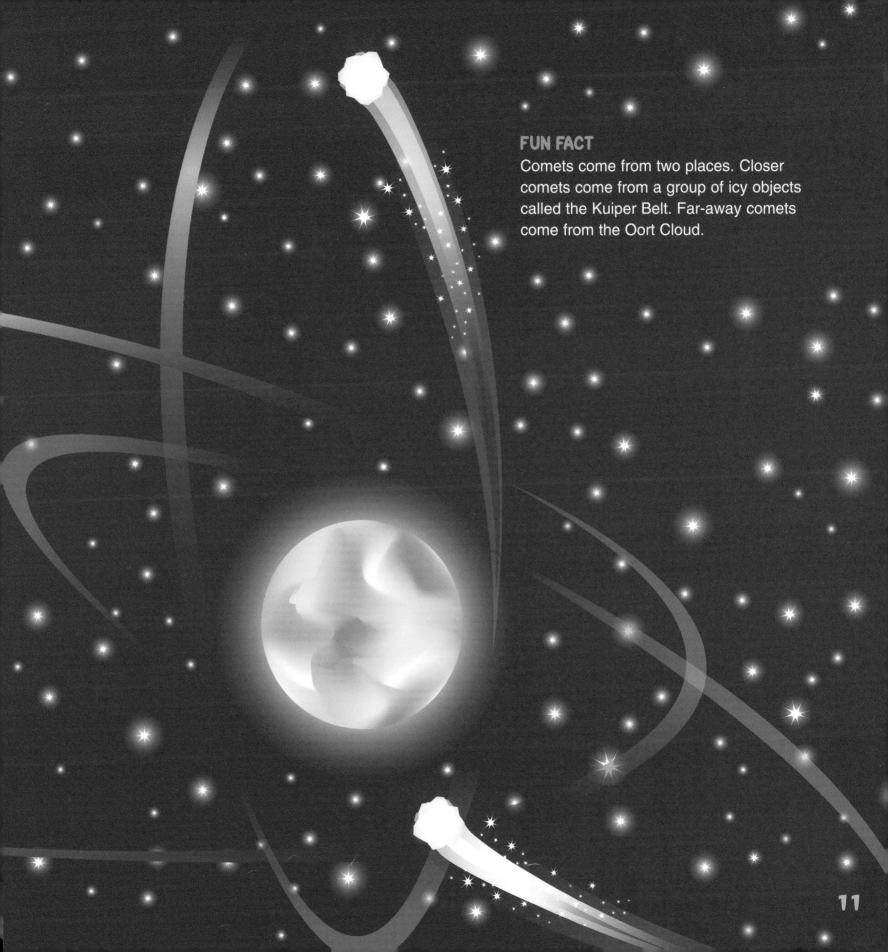

FUN FACT
Comets come from two places. Closer comets come from a group of icy objects called the Kuiper Belt. Far-away comets come from the Oort Cloud.

Two Tails

A rabbit's tail is small and fluffy. A tiger's tail is long and striped. Did you know comets have two tails?

Comets are mostly ice, but they're also made of dust and little bits of rock. They are sometimes called dirty snowballs. When a comet gets close to the sun, the heat of the sun makes the comet form tails. One tail is made of dust. One tail is made of gas.

FUN FACT

The tails of a comet form because of solar wind. The sun is always sending out a super-hot breeze. When a comet gets close to the sun, the sun blows on it. The heat melts the ice and makes the gas and dust trail after the comet like tails.

FUN FACT
Earth is hit with more than 100 tons
(91 metric tons) of space rock every day.

Space Rocks Come to Earth

Imagine you are munching on a cookie while having a picnic. You might drop some crumbs on the ground.

Comets and asteroids also drop crumbs. These small bits of space rock are called meteoroids. Sometimes Earth passes through the orbits of these meteoroids. Some even hit Earth.

Protecting Earth

You wear a helmet when you ride a bike. Your helmet protects you if you fall. Earth has protection, too.

A layer of hot gases surrounds Earth like a blanket. This layer is called the atmosphere. When meteoroids hit the atmosphere, they get very hot. Most meteoroids burn up and never hit the ground.

FUN FACT

A meteoroid burning up in the atmosphere is called a meteor. A meteor shower is a lot of meteors burning up all at once.

Meteorites and Craters

Not all meteoroids burn up. Some meteoroids do land on Earth. A meteoroid that hits the ground is called a meteorite.

Some meteorites are the size of small stones, but others are the size of huge boulders. When a large meteorite hits the ground, it makes a crater. Craters are deep, wide holes in the ground.

FUN FACT
Earth is not the only planet with craters. Mercury has a lot of craters. The Earth's moon is also covered with many craters.

Safe on Earth

You do not need to worry about space rocks crashing to Earth. Very few ever hit the ground. If a large one did get close, people would know it was coming.

Earth's gassy layer keeps us safe. We can watch the glowing chunks of ice, rock, and dust and be glad there are so many leftovers to enjoy.

FUN FACT

About every thousand years, Earth is hit with a meteorite about the size of a football field. It causes great damage to the area it hits.

Comet Tails

What you need:

* styrofoam ball
* popsicle stick
* two streamers
* tape

What you do:

1. Push the popsicle stick part way into the bottom of the styrofoam ball. The popsicle stick will be the handle. The ball will be the comet.

2. Tape two streamers to the ball—one on each side. One is like the dust tail. The other is like the gas tail.

3. Holding the comet by the handle, run in a wide open space.

4. What happens to the comet's tails? Which direction do they point while you are running? How is this like the solar wind?

Leftover Stuff

Learning from Rocks

Meteorites can tell us a lot about the solar system. When they land on Earth, they can teach people about what is floating in space, what other planets might be made of, and what our solar system was like long ago.

Largest Meteorite

The largest known meteorite is in Hoba, Namibia. It weighs about 60 tons (54 metric tons).

Is Pluto a Planet?

Pluto is a ball of rock and ice. It is the only icy planet. It is also close to the Kuiper Belt, a home to many comets. Some people believe Pluto should be called a comet instead of a planet.

Halley's Comet

Halley's Comet, named after Edmund Halley, comes close enough to Earth to see in the sky every 76 years. You might be able to spot it, but you'll have to wait until 2061.

Shrinking Comets

Every time a comet gets close to the sun, some of its ice melts away or its dust falls off. It grows smaller and smaller and will someday break apart.

Glossary

asteroids—pieces of rock and metal that orbit the sun
atmosphere—the layer of gases that surround Earth
comets—balls of ice, gas, and bits of dust
craters—large holes in the ground caused by crashing rocks
meteor—a meteoroid burning up in Earth's atmosphere
meteorite—a meteoroid that lands on Earth's surface
meteoroids—bits of rock or dust from a comet or asteroid
orbit—to travel around
solar wind—a hot breeze coming off the sun

To Learn More

At the Library

Birch, Robin. *Comets, Asteroids, and Meteors*. Philadelphia: Chelsea House, 2003.

Cole, Michael D. *Comets and Asteroids: Ice and Rocks in Space*. Berkeley Heights, N.J.: Enslow Publishers, 2003.

Rau, Dana Meachen. *Comets, Asteroids, and Meteoroids*. Minneapolis: Compass Point Books, 2003.

On the Web

FactHound offers a safe, fun way to find Web sites related to this book. All of the sites on FactHound have been researched by our staff. *www.facthound.com*

1. Visit the FactHound home page.
2. Enter a search word related to this book, or type in this special code: 1404811370
3. Click on the FETCH IT button.

Your trusty FactHound will fetch the best Web sites for you!

Index

Look for all of the books in the Amazing Science: Exploring the Sky series:

Fluffy, Flat, and Wet: A Book About Clouds
Hot and Bright: A Book About the Sun
Night Light: A Book About the Moon
Space Leftovers: A Book About Comets, Asteroids, and Meteoroids
Spinning in Space: A Book About the Planets
Spots of Light: A Book About Stars